# ———— CONTENTS ————

# Poetry Book Society

| | |
|---|---|
| CHOICE SELECTORS RECOMMENDATION SPECIAL COMMENDATION | JO CLEMENT & ROY McFARLANE |
| TRANSLATION SELECTOR | HARRY JOSEPHINE GILES |
| PAMPHLET SELECTORS | NINA MINGYA POWLES & ARJI MANUELPILLAI |
| CONTRIBUTORS | SOPHIE O'NEILL MEGAN ROBSON LEDBURY CRITICS |
| EDITORIAL & DESIGN | ALICE KATE MULLEN |

**Poetry Book Society Memberships**
Choice
**4 Books a Year:** 4 Choice books & 4 *Bulletins* (UK £65, Europe £85, ROW £120)
World
**8 Books:** 4 Choices, 4 Translation books & 4 *Bulletins* (£98, £160, £190)
Complete
**24 Books:** 4 Choices, 16 Recommendations, 4 Translations & 4 *Bulletins* (£230, £290, £360)
**Single copies of the *Bulletin*** £9.99

**Cover Artwork** Ranjeeta Kumari, *Poetry of Resistance*

ISBN 9781913129453 ISSN 0551-1690

Poetry Book Society | Milburn House | Dean Street | Newcastle upon Tyne | NE1 1LF
0191 230 8100 | enquiries@poetrybooksociety.co.uk
WWW.POETRYBOOKS.CO.UK

# LETTER FROM THE PBS

It is poetry prize season as I write, the Forward Prize shortlists have just been announced and when you receive this *Bulletin*, we should be just about to hear the winners. It's lovely to see that Mary Jean Chan's *Bright Fear*, is on the best collection shortlist alongside other PBS selected poets. And of course, we have the full shortlist for sale via our website at only £82.50 including free UK postage for members, or please give us a call and we can send you the bundle.

This season, we're thrilled to launch our new Digital Membership with Exact Editions. All PBS Members can enjoy free access to our inspiring digital *Bulletin* archive dating back to 2017 on their desktop, tablet or smartphone. You can find full details of how to register on the Members Area at www.poetrybooks.co.uk.

We're also partnering with Arji Manuelpillai's 'Poetry Pickle Jar' to create a special PBS Podcast. You can scan the QR code below to listen to the first episode featuring the wonderful Daljit Nagra on this season's choice, *Indiom*. Written in the style of a film script or epic poem, *Indiom* introduces the reader to the languages of Babu and Coolie English and the histories they contain.

Many of our selections this season delve into the past, exploring family and personal history – known, lost or potentially fabricated – the friction between first languages or mother-tongue and learnt English is explored too. Don't miss the must-have Special Commendation *Devotions*, the definitive collection from fifty years of Mary Oliver's writing. I can think of countless people I will gift this to.

It's such a thoughtful and entertaining round of selections – a big thank you to our selectors and poets. This is Harry Josephine Giles' last translation selection, so a huge thank you to Josie for their brilliant work sifting through an ever-growing list of translated submissions and picking some really remarkable books. We look forward to welcoming Shivanee Ramlochan as our Translation Selector for Winter.

SOPHIE O'NEILL
PBS & INPRESS DIRECTOR

# DALJIT NAGRA

Daljit Nagra has published four books of poetry with
Faber. He is Professor of Creative Writing at Brunel
University, Chair of the Royal Society of Literature,
Council of Society of Authors and a PBS Next Generation
Poet. Daljit has won the Forward Prize for Best Single
Poem and Best First Collection, the South Bank Show
Decibel Award and the Cholmondeley Award, been
shortlisted for the Costa Prize and twice for the T.S. Eliot
Prize. He is the inaugural Poet-in-Residence for Radio
4 and 4 Extra and presents the weekly *Poetry Extra*. His
poems have appeared in the *New Yorker*, the *LRB*, the
*TLS*, the *FT* and the *Guardian*.

# INDIOM

FABER   |   £14.99   |   PBS PRICE    £11.25

Anthony Burgess' *Clockwork Orange* brought us Nadsat spoken by the droogs. Dylan Thomas brought us *Under Milk Wood* set in an imaginary Welsh seaside village called Llareggub. Daljit Nagra's *Indiom* explores Babu and Coolie languages. It is set in Bulbul Hall, Charsovee, where a film crew watches a group of Anglo-Indian poets in a workshop; a global, eclectic and diverse gathering engaging with Nissim Ezekiel's Babu poem, 'Goodbye Party for Miss Pushpa T.S.'

Let's begin with Mr Common reciting from his own poem, which I believe is a gateway into *Indiom*:

> What words go old-boot lost in the desert like
>     tiger cries
> for rain sound? What handicraft way with sense
>     can untie us

Something lost is often replaced by something that binds us and to what extent does language free or hold us down? *Indiom* releases us from all those constraints. *Indiom* also engages with the English canon, bearing in mind all colonised subjects of Empire would be schooled and taught, by rote, the English Classics as the centre of all literature.

I want to believe in what Homi K. Bhabha calls a space where cultures collide and create something new, *Indiom* is that space. Relish its nuances, beauty and bravery. This is heavy with Babu tongue, Nissim Ezekiel, the writer at the beginning, is so important to the whole idea of kavya (epic poetry):

> ...gulping a glass of nimboo panee, 'When I give full clout
> to my accent kavyas, yes, there were the ones the crowds loved,
> but my peers hate them. I wrote my verse based on what I heard,
> is that wrong? Is that arrogance – is that empire hauteur?'

This is a book that should prickle us, as Derek Walcott said when looking at the words "Ashanti" and "Warwickshire," "both separately intimating my grandfathers' roots, both baptizing this neither proud nor ashamed bastard, this hybrid, this West Indian." *Indiom* flagrantly flounces in all its fluent babuness and the beauty of being Indian.

| SELECTOR'S COMMENT    ROY McFARLANE

# DALJIT NAGRA

During 2016, I decided to desist writing the standard thirty line poem and for the following three years I shunned the lyric muse till I found a project that could ignite me into a complex place. The novelist G.V. Desani and the poet Nissim Ezekiel got me thinking about Babu English. Their work that engaged with Babu English caused red faces for the educated Indians who spoke Babu English. In my text, I take this Babu English seriously, I make a virtue of this eccentric style as I do of Coolie English. I try to assess if they, having endured for well over a century, could be among the future voices of global English.

Babus and Coolies? During the Raj, the British needed administrators in India so they created a class of Babus. Their education included the Classics and the English canon. Yet English was merely the office language of these Babus. This might partly explain their macaronic English when written or spoken. Coolie English was a spoken form of the illiterate who knew the bare bones of English to help them get by. In *Indiom* my cast of characters, depending on their background, speak high, middle or low Babu English, Coolie English and one character is even credited with speaking Baboolie!

My first language was Punjabi and I learnt English at school, so I wanted to experiment with setting, to capture that uprooted yet jubilantly free feeling of excess I often experience as an inbetweener. In the spirit of Babu, the text that has transpired is a talkie that's written as a kind of play script though it reads perhaps like a dramatic poem. It is a mock-epic, a panegyric with end-rhyme and often in fixed syllables using Indian metrics alongside western poetic forms. Thank you PBS Selectors for liking *Indiom*.

## DALJIT RECOMMENDS

Erín Moure, *Kapusta* (House of Anansi Press); Alison Whittaker, *Blackwok* (Magabala Books); Sharon Thesen, *Refabulations: Selected Longer Poems* (Talon Books); Alexis Pauline Gumbs, *Spill* (Duke University Press); Vivek Narayanan, *Life and Times of Mr S* (HarperCollins); M. NourbeSe Philip, *Zong!* (Silver Press); Liz Howard, *Infinite Citizen of the Shaking Tent* (Penguin); Sawako Nakayasu, *Texture Notes* (Letter Machine Editions); Dennis Lee, *UN* (House of Anansi Press).

PBS CHOICE

# CANTO 1

PROLOGUE on Babus & Coolie languages, & how Nissim Ezekiel's poem 'Goodbye Party for Miss Pushpa T.S.', written in Babu English, caused offence on publication in 1970s India.

*Screenwriter's Companion lowers a book & speaks into the camera*

Salutations. Hi, I'm sat by greenwood tree in kameez
& Jodhpur. I'm sate as Ms Barrett Browning who once say,
she eat, she drink so much of classics from under a tree,
  so much that her head ache!

In this break from my 'eat & drink', our screenwriter ask for *ars
poetica* to announce her talkie, aka film.
They said, to disclose the gist that might aid the baat – the yarn,
  but in Standard English.

*Screenwriter's Companion gulps at the thought of attempting Standard English*

But first, I'd mention the Victorians who sought civil
servants to run the Raj – these were Babus; the Coolie was
the skivvy. Today's talkie imagines how their English
  endures in modern verse.

I'm sure you'd also adore knowhow of some lingo terms.
Indioms flow from the mood engagement between English
& Indian. Babu & Coolie are both indioms.
  Babu is eccentric

use of indioms. So high Babu is a lavish play
for least 'actual' speech. Meanwhile, Coolie's an oral record
from the unschooled, & low mix of indioms may embrace
  excessive Indic words.

*Screenwriter's Companion raises their script, clears the throat then recites an 'ars poetica'*

Monthly poetry groups flourish over world giving best
counsel, inspiration & samosa. Today's writing
group, in March 2020, is no different except
  the hill station setting –

is it in India? These Indic-heritage poets,
of whom but-not-one earn their crust in Ind, gather monthly
from over the globe. This month, they're in Bulbul Hall,
    which sits
            in the vale – Charsovee.

Today's theme is about a poem published five decade
distant by our 'Englisch Langwidge' poet from Ind, Mr
Nissim Ezekiel, you know him? P.S. quote was made
        by that great pretender

Mr Pound, of Mr Eliot's *Wasteland*. Nissim's lay
was for a fellow of his committee – she was leaving,
back in '70s, for good. Sad story? The lay was gay!
        Beaming Babu English.

'Badmash - his new poem! Is, he think, how we perorate!?'
It's how most felt mocked while sat under punkah, including
the lass in his lines! Today's poets will assess the fate
        of all such corruptings.

Oh so exciting! Will they go cut-throat barrack for high
drama in defence of Babu verse, or troop for groupthink;
a porcupine's test – get close as a hug till the pricks bite
        or, 'let's hold back for quilled

stimulus – we're comrades in one individual soul'.
Furthermore, as I've said, Babus were administrators
nurtured by men from the Atlantic Archipelago.
        These sahibs were masters

of the Babu, the Babu in turn mastered the Coolie.
Dear viewer, to add, please put aside your traditional
& classically trained methods. Our sensibility's
        an odd conceptual

double-helixing of the houses where we take our lease...

# JEN CAMPBELL

Jen Campbell grew up by the sea in the northeast of England. She is an award-winning poet and bestselling author of twelve books for adults and children, spanning fiction, non-fiction, poetry and picture books. She won the Jane Martin Poetry Prize, an Eric Gregory Award, and the Spelt Poetry Competition 2022 for her poem 'The Hospital Is Not My House' from *Please Do Not Touch This Exhibit*. She also works as a freelance editor, book reviewer and disability advocate. She currently lives in London. Find out more at www.jen-campbell.co.uk.

# PLEASE DO NOT TOUCH THIS EXHIBIT

BLOODAXE BOOKS   |   £10.99   |   PBS PRICE £8.25

Jen Campbell opens up with an epigraph by Ali Smith on what winter is. "An exercise in adapting yourself to whatever frozen or molten state it brings you". *Please Do Not Touch This Exhibit* is adapting to disabilities and chronic illness and celebrating the normality of it, she sings to the sea, the rain, the grass, to mythologies.

In 'Anatomy of the Sea,' we begin with the rain that falls across Northern England after the nuclear disaster of Chernobyl in April 1986 and a year later Campbell, as well as many others, are born with limb differences. "She speaks of a rage because the April before I arrived, / men were godlike in their mistakes. // Obsessed with their creations." And what Victorians would have called "monstrous" before the 1800s, she calls...

Now my hands are       birds
                               elephants
                               rock salt
                               constellations
                               anemone.

The heart of the collection is the sequence of 'The Hospital Is Not a Place...' these are beautiful tightly housed prose poems exploring her relationship with hospitals, "she speaks to the eyes directly. She locates their little ear drums and manages to charm them." The imagery is sublime, almost like Guillermo del Toro's *Pan's Labyrinth*, magical, conjuring sanctuaries for truth and joy in the midst of horrors, pain and the unbelievable.

Campbell brings us back to reality with epistolary from her childhood medical notes, about her operations and the almost freak show voyeurism of her journey. In this collection the monsters are not the ones trapped in the labyrinth but the ones on the outside. The ones who have created disasters such as Chernobyl and the insensitive female doctor giving her advice regarding IVF.

After the rain, there's a sweet smell, a petrichor of womanhood, desire for having children and hats. 'The Body Festival' says it all. "The carnival is here, you eat / it up like candy floss."

ROY McFARLANE

# JEN CAMPBELL

I was born nine months after Chernobyl, and geneticists told my parents that's why I was born disabled (there was a noted increase in babies born with limb differences in the northeast of England in the years after 1986). Whether Chernobyl actually had any part to play is something no one could prove, but it became the lore. If I'd been born a hundred years previously, doctors would have told my mother that I, (crudely called) a Lobster Child, was born that way because she'd eaten shellfish while pregnant. At that time, medically, I would also have been labelled "a monster."

Science changes; words evolve. As a disabled person, I have always been interested in bodies of text: in embodying words, trying them on for size, splicing them, discarding them. Looking at how words can shape a body, especially one that's been crafted through surgery.

It's an odd thing to step outside of yourself and look back on the metamorphosis of your own body. Having disfigurements, I'm so used to being observed by other people, so used to being on display in one form or another but, in recent years, going through IVF as a disabled adult, I have been forced to sit with the body of my childhood. I'd never really allowed myself to do that before: go through medical notes and memory-doors. I'd never granted myself time to gather all the pieces and peer at them gently. When I did, all at once, I felt I was an adult, a child, a medical observer, a folklorist, a seamstress, a bewildered storyteller; so many different people stitched at the hip and looking to each other for answers.

*Please Do Not Touch This Exhibit* is an attempt at answers. It's an excavation of body: body as house, body as story, body as animal.

## JEN RECOMMENDS

Nin Andrews, *Why God Is a Woman* (BOA); Raymond Antrobus, *The Perseverance* (Picador); *Stairs and Whispers* anthology (Nine Arches Press); Hannah Hodgson, *Where I'd Watch Plastic Trees Not Grow* (Verve Poetry); Lee Hyemi, *Unexpected Vanilla* (Tilted Axis); Ae Hee Lee, *dear bear* (Platypus); Bhanu Kapil, *How to Wash a Heart* (Pavilion); Cynthia Miller, *Honorifics* (Nine Arches Press); Jason Allen-Paisant, *Thinking with Trees* (Carcanet); Anita Pati, *Hiding to Nothing* (Pavilion); Sara Woods, *Sara or the Existence of Fire* (Horse Less Press).

I RECOMMENDATION

13

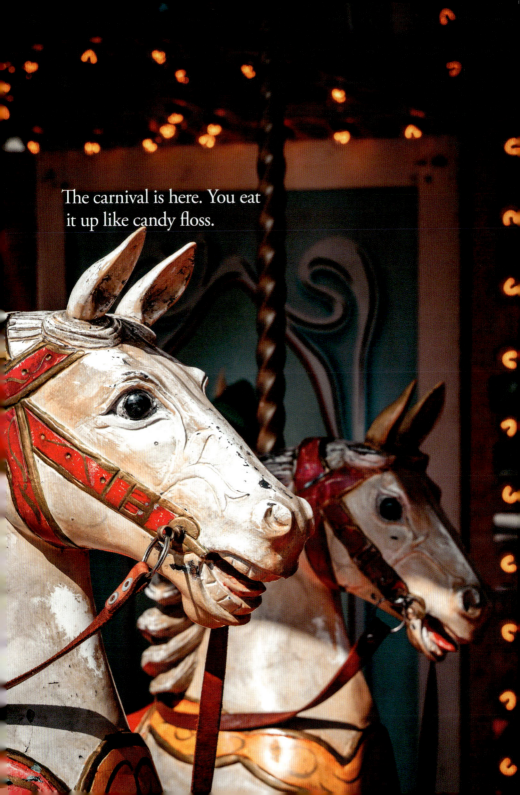

The carnival is here. You eat
it up like candy floss.

# AT FIRST, THE HOUSE IS BLUE

I don't think I need to explain
that it is winter as I approach the house.

The blue curtains don't just cover
the windows, they also curtain the grass.

The lawn leaks. It's waterlogged felt,
and walking across it is licking

velvet. I wouldn't recommend it, but
it is the only way to reach the house —

this house with its blue door and its blue
brain, which (if I had to) I would draw

as a sea of traffic lights — or perhaps
as some kind of whale.

# MARY JEAN CHAN

Mary Jean Chan is the author of *Flèche* (Faber, 2019) which won the Costa Book Award for Poetry and was shortlisted for the International Dylan Thomas Prize, the John Pollard Foundation International Poetry Prize, the Seamus Heaney Centre First Collection Poetry Prize and a Lambda Literary Award. Chan co-edited the anthology *100 Queer Poems* (Vintage, 2022) with Andrew McMillan. Chan serves as a Senior Lecturer in Creative Writing (Poetry) at Oxford Brookes University and is the recipient of the 2023-24 Judith E. Wilson Poetry Fellowship at the University of Cambridge. They are currently a judge for the 2023 Booker Prize.

RECOMMENDATION

# BRIGHT FEAR

FABER | £10.99 | PBS PRICE £8.25

If Mary Jean Chan's needle-like debut *Flèche* (Costa Poetry Prize, 2019) is a book of love poems, then its follow-up concerns separation. *Bright Fear* tentatively lifts the poet's fencing mask and declares their diaphanous, intersectional identity: "each year, I migrate between / cities and selves" ('How It Must Be Said'). Three compelling sequences shift between Hong Kong and England to uncover the ways that bigotry and expectation damage and suppress lives. They ask, as in 'Ars Poetica III':

What does it feel like to not have to hide things like
a small splinter of sadness or an even smaller need?

Concealments ache from page to page. Along with a lover, queer identity is banished to an Air B&B for a parental visit ("fireworks on the tongue"). The first of three 'EDI for Migrants' poems sees an academic respond "softly and politely" to the chuckling online moderator who wrongly assumes the speaker is "joining / the call from China". From a child's at-home quarrel with performed gender roles ('Glance') to a stranger's absurd question in The Poetry Café ('Answer'), seemingly safe spaces prove hazardous:

| | |
|---|---|
| try harder | depression |
| does not | exist |
| in families | like ours |
| trust | the doctor |
| if he is | your father |

Poems such as 'imperfection's school' remind us that disinformation can emanate from even the most trusted sources. Until 1990, the World Health Organisation wrongfully classified homosexuality as a psychological disorder. Chan navigates the punishing legacy of this unsound prescription, "travelling back- / and-forth" between instinct and instruction. These fiercely intimate lyric poems do "the hard / work of mending or mourning / what remains dear" ('Ars Poetica XII') with the most understated and highly admirable hope. *Bright Fear* invites readers to stand in solidarity and to recognise that ongoing "debates" on queer human rights are yet another manifestation of "the quotidian tug- / of-war between terror and love".

# MARY JEAN CHAN

For most of 2020, I found myself bereft of language. I couldn't read much, let alone write. During this period of collective grief, I found myself wondering what poetry was for in a time of crisis. I began jotting down images which felt like powerful metaphors for what poems meant to me: W.S. Graham's "constructed space", Mary Ruefle's "wandering little drift of unidentified sound", Anne Carson's "high blue room", Elizabeth Bishop's "inscrutable house" and Robert Hayden's "austere and lonely offices", to name but a few.

It was during the spring of 2021 that these ruminations began coalescing into what is currently the central poetic sequence of my second book *Bright Fear*, titled 'Ars Poetica'. This sequence of sixteen poems is bookended by sections respectively titled 'Grief Lessons' and 'Field Notes on a Family'. Some of these poems extend and develop themes which first appeared in my debut *Flèche*; others chart new ruptures and reconciliations which feel pertinent to my life. I found myself delving deeper into my complex relationship to language: English, as well as my mother tongue, Cantonese. I listened to Cantopop on repeat, from classics by Leslie Cheung to more recent work by Hong Kong singer-songwriters such as Yoyo Sham which helped me tune further into the sonic reverberations between words.

My stint in Singapore as a 2022 Visiting Writer at the Asia Creative Writing Programme and time spent in Hong Kong (HK) with family and friends also helped me grapple with deep-seated and pressing questions surrounding home and belonging. In my prose poem 'How It Must Be Said', I write: "For over a decade, I have taken what I could bear from the source text and discarded the rest. What do you miss most about HK? A childhood friend asks. Cantonese, I say. How it sounds like summer rain."

## MARY JEAN RECOMMENDS

Anthony (Vahni) Capildeo, *Like a Tree Walking* (Carcanet); Valzhyna Mort, *Music for the Dead and Resurrected* (Bloomsbury); Victoria Adukwei Bulley, *Quiet* (Faber); Will Harris, *Brother Poem* (Granta); Sarala Estruch, *After All We Have Travelled* (Nine Arches Press); Safiya Kamaria Kinshasa, *Cane, Corn & Gully* (Out-Spoken); Chen Chen, *Your Emergency Contact Has Experienced an Emergency* (Bloodaxe); Zaffar Kunial, *England's Green* (Faber); René Char, *Selected Poems*, ed. Mary Ann Caws and Tina Jolas (New Directions); Mary Ruefle, *Dunce* (Wave Books).

# LOVE FOR THE LIVING

What does it mean to want to live? Only this:
to refuse to see the mouth's anguish as a sign

to step out of an open window. To refuse to be
thirty and afraid of leaving one city for another.

To refuse to be a bomb shelter for your mother's
fears. What is it like to believe the years are not

a life sentence for bodies like yours? Like this:
a spiral of rainbow bunting sprung like relief

across a lit sky. The ache when your father
mentions your partner's name. How you'd

notice, incredulous, the way no one cares as
you stand in the open, holding her, kissing.

# POSTSCRIPT

in the penultimate scene where mother
and child are listening to one another

speak in spite of everything the way
an orchestra might play on bravely

even when the audience claps before
it's time you will want to stay awhile

in subtropical winter heat as sunlight
blazes through the fog of memory you

begin to wonder if the origin story can
at last be transfigured into the version

redacted through the centuries (the one
in which the garden comes alive) a queer

child's vision of paradise where the trees
are free to bear their multitudinous light

# TERRANCE HAYES

Terrance Hayes is the author of numerous books including *Lighthead* (2010), winner of the National Book Award, and *American Sonnets for My Past and Future Assassin* (2018), a finalist for the T.S. Eliot Prize, the National Book Critics Circle Award for Poetry, the National Book Award for Poetry and the Kingsley Tufts Poetry Award. His honours include a National Endowment for the Arts Fellowship, a Guggenheim Fellowship, and a 2014 MacArthur Fellowship. He lives in New York City, where he is a Professor of English at New York University.

# SO TO SPEAK

PENGUIN          |          £12.99          |          PBS PRICE £9.75

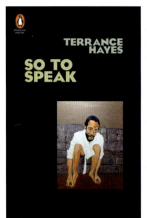

In the Deep South. A bird may eat a tree frog.
A fox eat the bird. A wolf may eat the fox.
And the wolf, then, may carry varieties of music
And cunning in its belly as it roams the countryside.

'Pseudacris Crucifer,' leads us into varieties of music carried in the belly of *So To Speak* as Hayes roams America or America could be the wolf, belly full of diverse people, histories and atrocities, roaming time. It doesn't matter, this is an inner vision of America where the narrator sings like a tree frog.

Hayes is the master of layered, interwoven conversations with fire in the belly, voltas and a magician's sleight of hand. Who else would lend Stevie Wonder the eyes of James Baldwin and Audre Lorde and claim, "Odds are ten / To one God also prefers to be referred to as They & Them", spend time with a homeless person who sings Purple Rain and then take you back to church for a public service announcement?

This is a public service announcement.
Mark your calendars. Tomorrow loves you.

'DIY Sestina' is a sestina of ekphrastic poems; please take time to consume these words and paintings as if you were standing under the Sistine Chapel or by the Murals at The Church of the Advocate in North Philadelphia. And muse with the quatrains of 'The Kafka Virus Verses: Thursday' which were written during the pandemic:

The madness of each ordinary day versus
the language of someone raised by history
versus someone raised by a virgin.
I'm mostly interested in the devil's story,

Whether it be the devil's story; the personal, memories of grandma and her "holy unholy rattle of wiring" or the universal story of the Boll Weevil "just a-looking for a home", *So To Speak* places everyone around the master's table so that we can hear all their stories and maybe one day dismantle the master's house.

# TERRANCE HAYES

More than inspiration, I am compelled by generative practice. *So to Speak* is the result of a regular practice of "keeping a record". The poems are a record of witness. I organized the book into three movements of "watching", as a figure of observation, as a kind of looking and reading. This book is the result of a core daily practice of watching and making poems. It is the result of a variety of exercises to grow and stay in shape. I think of the Do-It-Yourself sestinas as literal exercises a reader might undertake in a poetic practice. I hope the poems speak for themselves. If music is poetry's great analogue, I write for someone who listens to every channel, every style, every frequency on the radio. I am grateful for any and every reader of contemporary poetry. More than the dressing of my own poems, I offer a quick list of books I'd recommend from the last year or two, which includes:

1. Karisma Price's *I'm Always so Serious* (Sarabande). Her debut offers masterful portraits, mercurial testimonies and verbal inventions of an imminent poet of the new school/south, the next generation. Price speaks as someone raised on a gumbo of James Baldwin and James Booker, Buckjumping and Brooklyn. She speaks directly to and for you while speaking distinctly for herself.

2. Robert Wood Lynn's *Mothman Apologia*, winner of the 2021 Yale Younger poets Prize. This is not your typical narrative debut.

3. Imogen Xtian Smith's *stemmy things* (Nightboat) was another wonderful rereading. I've read Smith's brilliant collection half a dozen times, finding some unexpected texture, some slippery new layer at every turn. The magnificent Imogen Xtian Smith sticks tongues and fingers in earholes, pigeon holes, rabbit holes, pillage holes – any holes that need feeling.

4. Leslie Sainz's *Have You Been Long Enough at Table* (Tin House) probes spirituality with the verve and vitality of Emily Dickinson, if Dickinson had been born a Cuban American at the end of the last century. The narratives ring with the integrity of memoir and the inventiveness of allegory. This is a poet who has been long at the table, listening to the poetry of culture and family.

5. This past year I selected Simon Shieh's poems in a first book contest. His debut *Master*, forthcoming from Sarabande, is as merciless and restrained as a Rottweiler holding butterflies in its mouth, as steady and steely as a muzzle holding an artillery color. Violence grapples with forgiveness; kindness grapples with wickedness. This is a poetics of urgency rooted in the poet's mind and body.

**You can read more of Terrance's Recommendations on our PBS Blog.**

I RECOMMENDATION

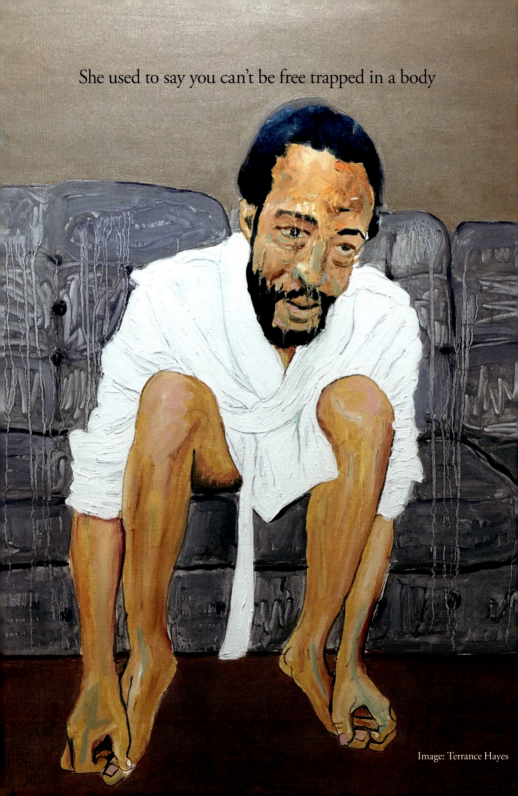

She used to say you can't be free trapped in a body

Image: Terrance Hayes

# AMERICAN SONNET FOR MY PAST AND FUTURE ASSASSIN

The only single women widows now or brides
Half married to the breeze. We lie to stay together.
We lie to make do. We lie to break the truth
Apart. We lie to shake fruit from the trees.
My mother favored the worker bee, her love buzzed
With stickiness & sting. I'm here about the widow
Afraid of butterflies. A widow knows ruin may be
As comprehensive as "rain," a kind of cover
For the dirt about the dead. Nature does not destroy,
Only change. Get down on your knees & pray
And get up quickly & live to celebrate that.
Falling is the first & most important skill in many things.
How to fall without breaking as well as how to break.
Tell me what you pray when you are broken or break.

# JACQUELINE SAPHRA

Jacqueline Saphra is a poet, playwright and teacher. Her recent collections include *All My Mad Mothers*, shortlisted for the 2017 T.S. Eliot prize; *Dad, Remember You are Dead* (2019) and *One Hundred Lockdown Sonnets* (2021), all published by Nine Arches Press. *A Bargain with the Light: Poems after Lee Miller* (2017) and *Veritas: Poems after Artemisia* (2020) were published by Hercules Editions. Her most recent play *The Noises* was nominated for a Standing Ovation Award. She is a founder member of Poets for the Planet and teaches at the Poetry School.

# VELVEL'S VIOLIN

NINE ARCHES PRESS | £10.99 | PBS PRICE £8.25

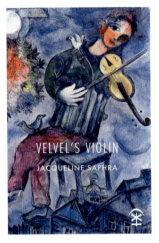

Testimony sits at the trembling heart of *Velvel's Violin*. As Nazis began to occupy Kołomyja in 1939, Rachel Shtibel's uncle buried his violin in a walnut tree's shadow. Her family of nine cramped into a shallow bunker scraped from the earth beneath an unlit barn, where for two years they prayed for liberation. Talking only in whispers, Shtibel, then a child, forgot how to speak. We learn why in the title poem:

> Their zayde witnessed, from behind the fence
> at the cemetery, his wife buried alive by the Gestapo.
>
> *The graves are moving, the graves are moving!*

Once in Poland, Kołomyja is today in the Ukraine, where over 40,000 people have fled the Russian invasion since 2022. In this fifth collection, T.S. Eliot Prize-shortlisted Jacqueline Saphra reels between the territory's troubling past and present with disbelief. 'The Moment a Russian Helicopter is Shot Down' flickers with reruns of what should be an unrepeatable history:

> I do not want to
> want to see this
>
> For god's sake
> I'm a pacifist
>
> I watch it eighteen times
> then put it on my favourites list

Savvy to deep media fakery and chocolates too good to be kosher, Saphra tackles fascist legacies with an acerbic wit. In the 'overheard on a train' trio, we meet an antisemitic passenger who delights in toxic gossip, spouting accusative conspiracies about Jewish complicity in acts of terror and state control. The longer poem 'Going to Bed with Hitler' is written after Volker Ullrich's biography, where the dictator's "detailed obsessions / bore me to death". Unafraid to hold a mirror up to those who spread hate and disinformation, Saphra is a poet at the height of her powers. She reminds us, as Holocaust survivor and Nobel Peace Prize winner Elie Wiesel once said, "whoever listens to a witness, becomes a witness".

I SELECTOR'S COMMENT

JO CLEMENT

# JACQUELINE SAPHRA

A collection, just like any individual poem, becomes its own process of discovery. As Robert Frost famously put it, "No surprise in the writer, no surprise in the reader".

I grew up in a secular, left wing household, and it was a determinedly Jewish one. To identify as culturally Jewish without the trappings or anchors of religion is simultaneously liberating and discomfiting. It feels impossible to disengage from my Jewishness and yet I don't know what it means; this was the starting point for the book, alongside my engagement with today's parallels of geopolitical turmoil, identity, prejudice and displacement.

I began by reaching out to my shrunken and scattered family for information but discovered mostly absences: even simple names of people and places were long buried and forgotten. I was left with the eradication wrought by the Holocaust, a few precious memories, some generalised reading and my imagination. I had just begun to plan a research trip to Eastern Europe in Spring 2022 when Russia invaded Ukraine; past and present seemed to be colliding and all my poetic plans fell apart.

It was then that I reminded myself to break free of my intentions, think like a poet and work with what I had. Thankfully *Velvel's Violin* resisted becoming a memoir, a family history, or a political treatise. Even my usual reliance on given forms as vessels to hold and mould the hottest content didn't work for me this time, and I had to find new formal strategies to explore the subject's polarities: kindness and cruelty, genocide and survival, despair and joy. The collection shaped itself into a chronicle of annihilation and absence but at the same time it insisted, to my surprise, on its role as a record of reclaimed stories, faith, connection, love and possibility.

## JACQUELINE RECOMMENDS

Jorie Graham, *To 2040* (Carcanet); Tom Sastry, *You have no normal country to return to* (Nine Arches Press); Terrance Hayes, *American Sonnets for my Past and Future Assassin* (Penguin); Ramona Herdman, *Glut* (Nine Arches Press); Tony Hoagland, *Priest Turned Therapist Treats Fear of God* (Bloodaxe); Anja Konig, *Animal Experiments* (Bad Betty); Imtiaz Dharker, *Postcards from God* (Bloodaxe); Edna St Vincent Millay, *Collected Poems* (Harper); Lucille Clifton, *Collected Poems* (BOA Editions); Charles Causley, *Collected Poems* (Picador); Margaret Atwood, *True Stories* (Cape) and *The Poetry of Yehuda Amichai* (FSG).

RECOMMENDATION

# THE PLAGUES ARE EVERYWHERE

*Passover 2020*

We gather round the plate, its song of songs
the history of birds on lilt and loop
of leaf and bloom, a blue of painted spring
to celebrate millennia of hope
against erasure. Did I say we *gather*?
Each in our little space, we make a grid
of faces. I feel I've loved you all forever.
For now, this is the closest we can get.
We work our shaky melody, we bear the weight
of memory and just for now, we're not alone.
The plagues are everywhere. We tell it straight,
we truly know it now. We fill our lungs
inhale some joy, exhale a kind of unison
singing with blue birds on a china plate.

# VELVEL'S VIOLIN

*After Rachel Shtibel*

All the years of the war, Velvel's violin lay silent
under the walnut tree where he'd buried it.

Like Rachel and Luci, their childhoods gagged
in barns and bunkers, all it wanted was to play.

Their zayde witnessed, from behind the fence
at the cemetery, his wife buried alive by the Gestapo.

*The graves are moving, the graves are moving!*
he told the ghetto, and lost the will to live.

When Rachel and Luci crawled out of the hole
they'd shared for two years, they had lost their voices.

After the war, the remnants of family disinterred
Velvel's violin from underneath the walnut tree.

*It is all we have left of Velvel* said their father
but of course nobody knew how to play it.

# MARY OLIVER

Born in a small town in Ohio, Mary Oliver published her first book of poetry in 1963 aged twenty-eight. Over the course of her long career, she received numerous awards. Her fourth book *American Primitive* won the Pulitzer Prize for Poetry in 1984. She led workshops and held residencies at various universities, including Bennington College, where she held the Catharine Osgood Foster Chair for Distinguished Teaching. She died in 2019.

# DEVOTIONS

CORSAIR | £30.00 HB | PBS PRICE £22.50

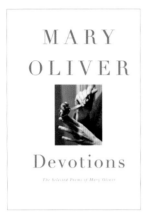

*Devotions* traces Mary Oliver's distinctive lyric voice over fifty-two years in print. Selected by the poet, this retrospective takes a pleasing reverse chronology. 'On Meditating, Sort Of' from *Blue Horses* (2014) invites readers to swim in the serene ponds of her later life:

> how wonderful to be who I am,
> made out of earth and water,
> my own thoughts, my own fingerprints
> all that glorious, temporary stuff

The compilation of this book is a revenant act that shares a curious intimacy with Oliver's dazzling *Dog Songs* (2013), in which we discover that her beloved pets chewed on scripture, attended writing workshops and placidly slept in her bed with paws in the air. From their "unshakable sleep", dead dogs come back bearing smiles and "dripping thick water, from the green bog" ('Her Grave'), as if they'd briefly slipped away from a walking trail. Oliver, too, has "come a great way" ('The First Time Percy Came Back').

In the Pulitzer Prize-winning *American Primitive* (1983) she buries stillborn kittens and uncomfortable truths with a characteristically Keatsian negative capability that leaves readers surprisingly serene, as in 'Skunk Cabbage':

> where the secret name
> of every death is life again — a miracle

The now infamous wild geese guide us to Oliver's earliest work: *No Voyage and Other Poems* (1963) which is concerned deeply by citizenship, spirituality and survival, subjects she returns to anew throughout this superb body of work. By tenderly communing with nature, her words offer remedies to begin "to sort the weeping ruins"('No Voyage') of a harsh and confusing world. Oliver's greatest gift is that she can "hear the almost unhearable" music amidst the noise. To walk through her sincere and remarkable poems is to share in this magic:

> If you have ever gone to the woods with me, I must love
> you very much.

| SELECTOR'S COMMENT    JO CLEMENT

# MORNING IN A NEW LAND

In trees still dripping night some nameless birds
Woke, shook out their arrowy wings, and sang,
Slowly, like finches sifting through a dream.
The pink sun fell, like glass, into the fields.
Two chestnuts, and a dapple gray,
Their shoulders wet with light, their dark hair streaming,
Climbed the hill. The last mist fell away,

And under the trees, beyond time's brittle drift,
I stood like Adam in his lonely garden
On that first morning, shaken out of sleep,
Rubbing his eyes, listening, parting the leaves,
Like tissue on some vast, incredible gift.

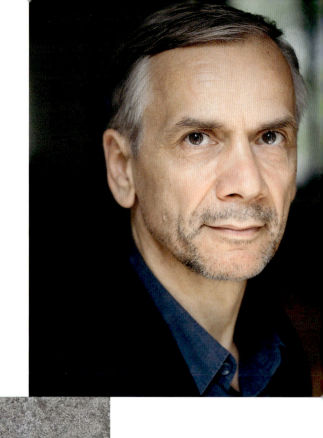

# LUTZ SEILER

---

# STEFAN TOBLER

Poet, novelist and essayist Lutz Seiler was born in Gera, Thuringia, in 1963 and today lives in Wilhelmshorst, near Berlin, and in Stockholm. After an apprenticeship in construction, he worked as a carpenter and bricklayer. Since 1997, he has been the literary director and custodian of the Peter Huchel Haus. His writing has won many prizes, including the Leipzig Book Fair Prize, the Ingeborg Bachmann and the German Book Prize, and been translated into twenty-five languages. His prize-winning second novel *Star 111*, his volume of non-fiction *In Case of Loss* and the poetry collection *Pitch & Glint* are published this year in English by And Other Stories. Some of his stories, poems and essays have appeared in *Modern Poetry in Translation*, *PN Review*, *Poetry*, *PROTOTYPE*, *The New Statesman*, *Shearsman*, *Stand* and *The White Review*.

Born in Belém, Brazil, to English and Swiss parents, Stefan Tobler is a translator and the founder of And Other Stories. Authors he has translated include Clarice Lispector, Raduan Nassar and Arno Geiger. He grew up in northern Brazil and southern England, and has now made his home in the Dark Peak.

TRANSLATION CHOICE

# PITCH & GLINT
## LUTZ SEILER, TRANS. STEFAN TOBLER
AND OTHER STORIES   |   £14.99   |   PBS PRICE £11.25

"Roads / need softly / rolling languages," writes Lutz Seiler in an exquisitely reflexive moment of this remarkable translation. The poems of *Pitch & Glint* cross between the industrial, rural and suburban landscapes of East Germany, following such roads, their languages, and their "slender animals here / that each evening / creep down the avenue".

Stefan Tobler's dense and precise translations seek out patterns of sound and sense that can convey, in English, some of the ecstatic music of the original. This passion is without illusion or romance, but rather arrives from a deep and familiar attention to the music of the world. That music is everywhere waiting to be found and made into poetry:

> what
>
> occurs is misted
> by the spittle of birds the ear
> asleep in oil the dead grow
>
> & die in the garden, silence
> is a vertical sleep.

Recording this music requires such fluid syntax, allowing sentences to slip over and under each other to make new meanings. The force of this music made me reconsider the values of the broad field of ecological poetry. At its best, the poetry of nature must uncover the intertwining of the human and the natural, and how each is found in the other. In Seiler's poetry, this mutual dependence is pursued into very human landscapes, where there is as much darkness as flame. Thus, "the suburb commutes under / the trees" and "from the sky above courtyards / pulverised swallows fall", while, in a later poem, "from under / the telegraph poles' tar-taping the fresh / beetles scrabble to the light". These juxtapositions neither praise or condemn: rather, they speak of the necessity of close attention to the presence of life and death in all places, all things. Roads need softly rolling languages, and so do we.

SELECTOR'S COMMENT

40    HARRY JOSEPHINE GILES

# MECHANICS OF THE PICTORIAL WORLD

taking down the swing
in autumn & putting it up
in April. day after day

the suburb commutes under
the trees and hour after hour
from the sky above courtyards

pulverised swallows fall & neatly
stuffed ones come up: the
gravity in their eyes hangs

raw as an egg
over the globe over
the man at the next table

(in sleep he leans his face
against the lamp) and over
the slender animals here

that each evening
creep down the avenue
& murmur

*ev'nin* into the dark as
if tucking the greeting away
in their warm almost

sleeping bodies

# DANE HOLT

Dane Holt was the winner of the inaugural Brotherton
Prize in 2019 awarded by the University of Leeds. In
2018 he was selected for *The Poetry Ireland* Introduction
Series. His poems have appeared in *Poetry Ireland Review,
The Trumpet, The White Review, Stand, bath magg, One
Hand Clapping, Anthropocene, Ink, Sweat and Tears, The
Manchester Review* and elsewhere. He is poetry editor of
*The Tangerine*, a Belfast magazine of new writing. He
recently completed a PhD at Queen's University, Belfast,
and is the current Ciaran Carson Publishing Fellow.

# MANY PROFESSIONAL WRESTLERS NEVER RETIRE

THE      LIFEBOAT      |      £6.50      |

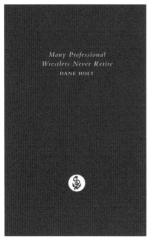

When I first flicked open this little book I was startled by the clarity and precision of its descriptive writing. Dane Holt spins a plethora of enchanting images, from the "windscreen shivering / like a cobweb" to the bodybuilders whose backs "were once wide as stingrays". It rings with the life blood of Levine and Simic while swinging between these tiny stories of real people bolstered to a somewhat mythical status.

Holt holds that wry, tongue-in-cheek charisma similar to Jonathan Edwards or Caroline Bird, the sort of poet that you'd love to hear tell a story in a bar. The sort of poet that makes words flow easily off the tongue, poking a smile from even the most jaded poetry fan. But these poems are rich in many other ways too.

A wrestling ring hangs as the backdrop for a series of investigations into masculinity. In these investigations the speakers hold their own, guiding us seamlessly from room to room where we are forced to observe a series of men in a variety of settings, which range from the mundane and strange, to the hopeless and frustrated, but all of them lean into their ridiculousness. From bodybuilders to novel writers, wrestlers to political canvassers, for me, the highlight was probably a dramatic monologue for John Cena.

> Often, when it comes to your
> distinctive brand of violence, John,
> less is more
> and none is more than enough.

Holt is a wonderful portrait poet, painting vignettes portraying characters with all their flaws and strengths in a fresh and nuanced light. These poems are quiet, subtle and careful. They carry with them a miraculous sense of soul and with that, they draw you in.

Recently, contemporary poetry has veered towards the more abstract, it dips its head into political farce and global crisis. However, this little book reminds me that poetry will always have a place to shine a spotlight on the everyday people in our society. It can remind us how strange our existences are and with that realisation, comes the knowledge that we are not that different after all.

ARJI MANUELPILLAI & NINA MINGYA POWLES

# MORE BOOTS

He'd struggle right now to pick up his life
and put it down somewhere worse.
From this distance he can't distinguish

tea from coffee. But there's something in his cup.
He sobbed at the meeting, begged the panel
not to send him again. The last thing he remembers

is a knock at the door, boots in his face
and balls, instructions, more boots.
At one point or another, everyone he's ever known

has lied to his face. He looks at the cat
who seems somehow relieved to be back
luxuriating in zero gravity.

DANE HOLT

# AUTUMN BOOK REVIEWS

## AMY ACRE: MOTHERSONG
### REVIEWED BY OLUWASEUN S. OLAYIWOLA

*Mothersong* contains no lullabies but sets its matrilineally anxious narratives to music. Embodying motherhood's often undisclosed moods – awe, disbelief, doubt – Acre untangles motherhood as the bedrock for other familial relations: "I know I am in here somewhere". Etymologically and autobiographically, *Mothersong* maps the poet's lushly imaginative worldview: "bears raining... cradle of river... black eye full of isn't." Acre loves the world and *Mothersong* is an artifact of that love.

AMY ACRE

Mothersong

SEPTEMBER | BLOOMSBURY | £9.99 | PBS PRICE £7.50

## DIONNE BRAND: NOMENCLATURE
### REVIEWED BY DAVE COATES

A journey through forty years of history and poetry, *Nomenclature* witnesses, among other things, the fall of revolutionary Grenada and Nicaragua, the sensationalisation of police violence and the West's perpetual warmongering. *Nomenclature* is an account of Brand's struggle to disrupt the brutality of her poems' subjects, to find something like beauty amid language's wreckage. This is a monumental achievement, a poet's ambition matched by its community of readers; Brand may be a touchstone for British poets for years to come.

JULY | PENGUIN | £16.99 | PBS PRICE £12.75

## FRED D'AGUIAR: FOR THE UNNAMED
### REVIEWED BY DAVE COATES

*For The Unnamed* is a creative exploration of an incident in 1852, when a black jockey – unnamed in the press – won a horse race that shook society in contemporary Los Angeles. The book ends beautifully, with deeply moving lyrics on the nature of blackness and recognition in America, but the middle section loses vital dramatic momentum. This collection shines in its more meditative pieces, but some of its historical import is lost among its comic diversions.

AUGUST | CARCANET PRESS | £14.99 | PBS PRICE £11.25

# LEDBURY CRITICS TAKEOVER

## SUSANNAH DICKEY: ISDAL
### REVIEWED BY MAGGIE WANG

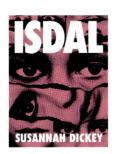

Writing about other people's lives and deaths is a risk; *ISDAL* takes it well. It is grisly but graceful, detailed in its imagery yet erudite and conceptually engaged. "In a city on Norway's coast there's a grave untouched by lineage. / A single member's club with hidden entry and no signage." The collection grows like a vine out of this grave. Yet, it is not obsessive. Rather than burying itself completely in a single story, a single mystery, it has its own rich voice and imagery.

SEPTEMBER | PICADOR | £10.99 | PBS PRICE £8.25

## WILLIAM LETFORD: FROM OUR OWN FIRE
### REVIEWED BY DAVE COATES

Letford's ambitious third book harnesses his sharply analytical and fiercely humane lyric imagination to stunning effect. Beginning with intimate and earthy portraits of a found family living off-grid, it gradually realigns like a magic eye puzzle into a compelling work of speculative fiction, a tense story of a gaggle of misfits attempting to repair their own – perhaps humanity's – fraught relationship to nature and each other. A gorgeous and heartbreaking story, a challenge to poetry's borders.

AUGUST | CARCANET | £14.99 | PBS PRICE £11.25

## EMILY ZOBEL MARSHALL: BATH OF HERBS
### REVIEWED BY SHASH TREVETT

A tender collection of loss and personal history which traces the poet "back to fields of cane" on Martinique. Here are poems which honour her progenitors, her mother Jenny, her partner, memorialising their "voices" as they float "on the breeze". Later, witty poems sit alongside those celebrating the Welsh or Yorkshire landscape: her riposte to a racist school bully, long delayed, is masterful. Marshall's skills with imagery shine in poems which shift shape "like shadows in the gloaming".

JULY | PEEPAL TREE PRESS | £9.99 | PBS PRICE £7.50

BOOK REVIEWS

## MOMTAZA MEHRI: BAD DIASPORA POEMS
### REVIEWED BY SHASH TREVETT

This searing collection should be read, digested and then read again, slowly. It is a manifesto on dislocation (from South to North, East to West, and back again), on forgetting, on the dangers of raising the motherland onto "sacrificial posts". It is peopled both by figures plucked from history and the everyday displaced, and dissects with scalpel-precision how they negotiate new borders and new stories. This is a collection which will leave you thinking and questioning: for "equilibrium is not a destination you can relocate to".

JULY  |  CAPE  |  HB £14.99  |  PBS PRICE £11.25

## MICHAEL PEDERSON: THE CAT PRINCE
### REVIEWED BY DAVE COATES

*The Cat Prince* is a glittering and charming miscellany. Like Billy Collins, Pedersen's poems generally summon a single image, situation, or thought, then dig into their vast bag of poetic tricks to turn it into something strange and shining. Though the book keeps focus, broadly, on boyhood and masculinity, its arrangement feels somewhat scattershot, and suffers a little from repetitiveness in its texture. Pedersen's ability, however, to keep a poem afloat with linguistic brio alone is unquestionable.

JULY  |  CORSAIR  |  £12.99  |  PBS PRICE £9.75

## NICOLE SEALEY: THE FERGUSON REPORT: AN ERASURE
### REVIEWED BY DAVE COATES

Across eight poems Sealey examines the habitual imposition of state violence, the struggle to retain one's humanity when it is officially denied. This is a meticulous, strikingly beautiful erasure that feels, like M. NourbeSe Philip's *Zong!*, like it has been painfully, painstakingly extracted, that the journey of the word to the page cost dearly. *The Ferguson Report* wrestles with the question of what can be said, when anything you say can and will be used against you.

SEPTEMBER  |  BLOODAXE  |  £12.99  |  PBS PRICE £9.75

## WILLIAM SIEGHART: THE POETRY PHARMACY FOREVER
### REVIEWED BY DAVE COATES

*The Poetry Pharmacy Forever's* winning formula presents a "condition" (love, loss, alienation) and a short poem as its cure. Sieghart regularly diagnoses the shallowness of modernity, but the book's critical engagement tends towards the skin-deep and social media-friendly. However ameliorative its intent, there is the risk that deeply complex and personal works of art are reduced to mere thoughts for the day, but *The Poetry Pharmacy* treads this line carefully and succeeds in making poetry accessible to a wider readership.

SEPTEMBER | PENGUIN | £14.99 | PBS PRICE £11.25

## RICHARD SKINNER: WHITE NOISE MACHINE
### REVIEWED BY MAGGIE WANG

Many of the poems in *White Noise Machine* read like song lyrics. Occasionally, they seem confined by their form, as the strictures of triolets and pantoums eliminate room for nuance: "Don't give up / 'Cause everybody hurts / When you're sure you've had enough / Sometimes everything is wrong." Still, the collection is far from bland. Rather, even as it focuses on sound, it is full of colour: "the seasons back-pedal–/ winter to autumn, gold to green... Then evening falls, clouds of pewter, / ash-bloom, carbon."

JUNE | SALT | £10.99 | PBS PRICE £8.25

## DAWN WATSON: WE PLAY HERE
### REVIEWED BY OLUWASEUN S. OLAYIWOLA

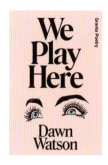

"I took a Twix. The wrapper was wet in my hand. / The next day, my dad was dead." Cinematically fast-paced and darkly detached, this is a masterful tone poem, consisting of story-memories from four young girls in North Belfast. Watson's short detective-like sentences are seductively propelling, though it's the silence around the speaker's dilemmas that pierce: "If you go by her house, you hear her dad / hit her and her mum. It's just the vacuum / blattering the walls, Max says." Suspenseful and unsentimental, this is page-turner poetics.

AUGUST | GRANTA | £12.99 | PBS PRICE £9.75

# AUTUMN PAMPHLETS

## FRED D'AGUIAR: ARBORETUM FOR THE HUNTED

The title poem of Fred D'Aguiar's *Arboretum for the Hunted* hauntingly memorialises victims of US police brutality, planting a tree for the "so many, too many, black people killed on account of their skin". Alongside these societal struggles sit poems about the poet's own personal struggle for survival against an aggressive form of cancer. D'Aguiar carefully "unpick(s) this stitched / dark" in a pamphlet which is marked by unexpected hope, deep emotion and observation: "all over with / seeing feeling".

ARC    PUBLICATIONS              |              £8.00              |

## JANE BLUETT: SHE WILL ALLOW HER WINGS

Jane Bluett's astonishing pamphlet spans formal verse, wry retellings, and moving pieces which give voice to women and celebrate women's words. Poems such as 'Elegy' appear simple at first glance, but reading them you feel a pull to dig for their deeper complexity, and are rewarded. This is an affecting blend of gentle observation and sharp-toothed humour, which only reveals its bedrock of grief as you journey through it.

FIVE    LEAVES              |              £7.00              |

## BETH FRIEDEN: ANCHOR IN THE LAND

Written in both Scottish Gaelic and English by an American immigrant in Scotland, *Anchor in the Land* is rooted in the "architexture" of place. Poems of dislocation, motherhood, anxiety and hope are anchored by linguistic revelry, as the poet riffs from "nebulous" to "nubile" and "jubilation" billows across the page. Even without understanding the facing Gaelic text, it is a joy to explore the shapes and sounds of this ancient tongue and see it brought back to life so vividly.

STEWED    RHUBARB    PRESS              |              £6.00              |

## OAKLEY FLANAGAN: G & T

*G & T* comprises a single poem which follows its narrator through a series of anonymous drink-fuelled nights and encounters with older men. Sections of dense prose poetry contrast with those which make use of sparseness and white space, and the poem is almost analytical in its approach to desire and the power structures involved in the performance and expression of sexuality. Forceful while touched by pathos, this is an accomplished debut.

OUTSPOKEN    PRESS         |         £8.00                    |

## JULIA ROSE LEWIS: NEARLY IDENTICAL SHARKS

In Julia Rose Lewis's strange and playful pamphlet, art and science, miracle, magic, equation and discovery all meet in poems comprised of language that is at once precise, as creatures and compounds are specifically named, and slippery, as sounds and letters slide around each other through spells and wordplay. Throughout these dynamic poems swim darker elements; sharks in the deep, a threat at the cellular level.

BROKEN   SLEEP   BOOKS         |         £8.99         |

## PRERANA KUMAR: IXORA

The "blinding vermillion" ixora flower blooms with violent persistence, almost prescience, throughout this debut pamphlet. There is violence too in family inheritance and domestic rituals, as the poet unravels "a knotted father thing". Kumar "slits the neck of her story", mapping the "migration pattern as cannibal" and the brown body "as a kind of bruising". Sticky with ceremony and memory, these poems are tender guavas to slowly unpeel and feast upon.

GUILLEMOT   PRESS            |            £8.00                |

PAMPHLET REVIEWS

# AUTUMN BOOK LISTINGS